香港國際詩歌之夜 *2011*
INTERNATIONAL POETRY NIGHTS IN HONG KONG

編輯 Editors

方梓勳 Gilbert C. F. Fong

陳嘉恩 Shelby K. Y. Chan

柯夏智 Lucas Klein

何潔賢 Amy Ho Kit Yin

北島 Bei Dao

姚風

Yao Feng

目錄 Contents

絕句（節錄）

全體會議上
舉起了三千隻右手
齊刷刷的
像是割草機修剪後的草坪

一隻春天的燕子
張開剪刀
從我的手臂上方飛過
我發出一聲慘叫

她被一個個男人傷透了心
除了愛耶穌
她誰也不愛
她不停地給他寫信

對她而言，在這個世界上
只有這個男人
在十字架上永遠愛着

In Brief (Extracts)

*

at the plenary meeting
three thousand right hands are raised
at the same level
like a lawn trimmed by a mower

a spring swallow
opened its scissors tail
flew past above my arm
I gave out a sad, shrill cry

*

her heart by men broken
though not by Jesus
she loves nobody
she keeps on writing him letters

he's the only man
in this world for her
always up on the cross
in the state of love

*

大師雙眼微合
氣沉丹田
然後走向沸騰的油鍋

大師舉手向天
好像抓住了一朵白雲
然後說
他已經油炸了天空

*

麥子在波浪中歌唱
低下頭顱
看見了鐮刀的鋒芒

一條花蛇沿着曲線逃逸
從城市狂奔而來的公路
把牠截成數段

六月，誰讓我去複習悲傷
刮雨器不停地向我告別
前方擋住了去路

*

the master narrowed his eyes
suspended his breath in the belly
came to the wok with boiling oil

he raised his hand to the sky
as if grabbing a cloud
and said
the sky's already fried

*

wheat sings in waves
heads down
regards the blaze of sickles

a flowery snake makes its wavy line getaway
the highway sprinting from the city
cuts the snake into pieces

in June, who's to review my sadness
the windscreen wipers bid endless farewells
blocking the road ahead

*

每天晚上從窗外向外望
都會看到那盞街燈
按時點燃自己，照亮別人

有一天它突然消失了
它一定是厭倦了這樣的生活
騎着電線杆
向沒有黑夜的地方奔去

*

許多西方知名品牌進駐中國
但也時常抱怨
說中國富豪的買家群體太不穩定
「客人一下子就消失了
要不然出了國
要不然就是進了監獄。」

*

大海裝滿無數滴水
有人告訴我
從一滴水中可以見到大海

在一滴大海中
我打撈沉船、銀幣和屍體

*

every night I looked out of the window
and saw that street lamp
lit to light others

one day it disappeared
tired of this life
it rides on a wire pole
bound for a place with no darkness

*

famous western brands
get themselves well into China
but still often complain
about the instability of rich Chinese customers
"They have vanished all at once
either gone abroad
or to jail."

*

the sea is holding innumerable drops of water
someone told me
the sea can been seen in a drop of water

in a drop of the sea
I salvage the sunk boats, silver coins and corpses

*

蒼茫暮色中
我凝視着紀念碑
一個英雄，從浮雕上走下來
向我借火點煙
一點光亮下，我看見
他那張欲言又止的臉

紀念碑亮如燈柱
挺立於夜空
從古至今，歷史
就是一抹光亮，就是幾張面孔
其餘的部分
由無邊的黑暗構成

*

世界並沒有改變
還是公事公辦

落日「嘭」地一聲
一枚公章
蓋在了地平線上

*

in the ashen dusk
I gazed at the monument
a hero came down from the bas-relief
asked me for a light
in that drop of light I saw
he wanted to say something
but on second thought
decided not to

the monument was as bright as a lamp post
standing in the evening sky
since ancient times, history
is a hint of light, is a few faces
the rest of it—
boundless dark

*

the world hasn't changed
official principles still apply

the sun set
bang!
an official chop
came down on the sky line

終於批准了
我望着窗外，就像一個黑夜
望着另一個黑夜

*

發明領帶
是在巴黎的冬天
當初是為了保暖

在炎熱的夏天
那個戴領帶的人
不停地顫慄

他把領帶擰成一根繩子
在屋樑上
懸成一個繽紛的圓

他説，必須親自去死
他是他的遺體

無論如何
他要參加自己的葬禮

finally it was approved
I looked out of the window, it was like
a dark night gazing at another dark night

*

the neck tie was invented
in a winter in Paris
at first it was for keeping warm

in the heat of summer
the man who wears a tie
felt the cold

he twisted the tie into a rope
hung from the beam
to make a colourful circle

he said he must die in person
he was his own remains

by whatever means necessary
he would go to his funeral

*

一隻中國的穿山甲
懼怕廚子和美食家
他鑽過廚房的水泥地面
穿過石頭和岩漿
最後抵達了
地球的另一端

現在，他在紐約一家西餐廳打工
並申請了綠卡

*

你的陽光背後
是我的黑夜
地球旋轉，改變睡姿
並不能改變夢的方向
焦渴，一個來自遠方的客人
還在嘴唇上跋涉
一個杯子在海上漂浮
想裝下整個大海
因為夢境
魚群躍出海面

*

in China a pangolin
was afraid of cooks and gourmets
so he made a hole and went through the kitchen's floor
stones and magma
and in the end
came to the other side of the world

now he's working in a French restaurant in New York
and has applied for a green card

*

what's behind your sunshine
is my dark night
the Earth spins, changing sleeping position
that won't change the dream's direction
terribly thirsty, a traveler from afar
presses on by lip
a cup floating in the sea
attempts to hold all
because there are groups of fish
jumping from the sea surface
in the dream

*

我的理想
是做一個建築師
是建一座三百層的政府大樓

官員們匆忙地進進出出
因為裏面沒有廁所

廁所
建在低矮的南區

*

地窖裏過冬的土豆
伸出有毒的手指
指揮春天的樂隊

一根被染黑的霜髮
絆倒了一頭白象

我們用死亡
發明了動詞

一頭被運往屠宰場的老牛
反芻自己的眼淚

*

my ambition
is to be an architect
to build a three-hundred-floor government building

the officials would have to go in and out in a hurry
because there would be no toilet inside

the toilet
would be built in the slum area in the city's south

*

the potato hibernating in the cellar
sprouts fingers
to conduct the music of spring symphony

a strain of grey hair dyed black
trips a white elephant

we've used death
to invent a verb

an ox sent to the slaughter house
is ruminating tears

*

脫掉一切可以脫掉的
我的淨重是七十公斤
這只是肉體
與心靈無關

而心靈沒有淨重
只有毛重
因為要加上黑暗
因為要加上廢墟

*

藝術家在廣場中央
豎起一座威武的銅馬像
既不屬於帝王
也不屬於將軍
藝術家想讓它屬於人民

每一個來到廣場的人
都想騎上去
每一個騎上的人
都顯得威風凜凜
擺出的姿勢
不是帝王，就是將軍

*

having taken off what I can
my net weight is seventy kilograms
this figure concerns only the flesh
has nothing to do with spirit

my spirit doesn't have net weight
but the gross kind
because it has to include the darkness
because it has to include those ruins

*

in the centre of a square the artist
set a mighty bronze equestrian statue
it belongs neither to kings
nor generals—
it's for the people

everyone who comes to the square
wants to ride on it
everyone who rides on it
looks majestic
the poses they strike
are either like those of kings or of generals

*

披上皮大衣
即使趴在地上，也不像狼
我像綿羊一樣睡着了

夢中走近你
狂吃身體上的青草
雪越下越大
但落在我身上的雪
我一點也看不見

*

在縣城
眼看着那個男人爬上橋頭
大罵了一聲甚麼
就跳了下去

只留下黑壓壓的指手畫腳
和七嘴八舌
而他一直沒有上來

水中央的漩渦
看起來像一個救生圈

*

having put on the fur coat
I don't look like a wolf when
I'm flat on the ground
I look like a sheep asleep

in the dream I came close to you
crazily ate the grass on your body
snow was falling more heavily
but whatever it was had fallen on me
I couldn't see

*

in the county town
I saw the man climbing
onto the end of the bridge
he let out a curse
and jumped

what remained were a crowd
of pointing fingers and talk
he never came out of the water again

the whirlpool in the centre
was like a lifebelt

*

手機傳來了
噩耗

去殯儀館的路上
堵車

*

大海心潮澎湃
但不會説海枯石爛

大海只會踮起腳尖
在嘴唇的高度
把礁石上的少女
抱在懷裏

*

我的身後，總跟着一個陰影
包裹着我的檔案
我不知道誰在填寫我的檔案
也不知道寫了些甚麼

*

the news of death
sent by cellphone

on the way to the funeral home
a traffic jam

*

the sea was choked up with emotions
but it wouldn't say "I'll love you
till the sea goes dry and the rocks dissolve"

the sea would only stand on tiptoe
to the height of the lips
and hug the young woman
on the reef

*

behind me, there was always a shadow
wrapping up my profile
I didn't know who was filling it in
or what had been written

從我搖擺不定的前程推測
我是檔案中的一個病句
被蒙面人反複修改
直到我向陰影開了一槍

*

在黃山，尋找
二十年前留下的連心鎖
卻不見蹤影
就像那段蒼茫的感情
已鎖進了風中
只有那棵迎客松站在雲海中
向我招手

而你不停地問
迎客松是真的嗎？

*

在B城的主要大街，常常看見
豪華轎車
懸掛着窗簾飛馳而過
裏面載着陰影般的秘密

from my fickle future, I presume
that there was an illiterate line
being edited over and over again
by a masked person
until I fired at the shadow

*

on Mountain Huangshan, searching for
the heart-linked-to-heart locket
I left behind twenty years ago
no trace could be found
as for the expansive feelings
locked up in the wind
in the sea of clouds
only the greeting pine
waved at me

you kept asking
if the greeting pine was real

*

on the main street of B city
grand cars can often be seen
curtains on the car windows
they speed along
their shadowy secrets

在一些國家，法律不允許遮擋車窗
哪怕在裏面做愛
也許他們講究透明度
就像在這裏，人民都活在明處

*

1898年
葡萄牙廢除了死刑
原因是
沒有人願做劊子手

這樣的歷史細節
比起達‧迦馬的航海壯舉
更讓我心生感慨
我扔掉了手中的血饅頭

*

歷史上，黃禍論甚囂塵上
西方人說，中國人像螞蟻一樣繁殖
是對人類不負責的表現

in some countries
car windows aren't allowed to be covered
not even when you want to make love inside
perhaps they are particular about openness
just like here
people live in places where all is very visible

*

in 1898
Portugal abolished capital punishment
the reason was
that no one wanted to be executioner

compared with Vasco da Gama's great deeds
this kind of historical detail
gets me deep down
I threw away the steamed bun stained with human blood

*

in history, the Yellow Peril is widely known
the westerners say Chinese multiply like ants
and that is irresponsible

這種指責，沒有影響中國人的生殖力
如果不是革命不是饑荒不是戰亂
不是瘟疫不是運動不是地震
不是洪水不是結紮不是礦難
中國的人口
比現在的還要多

我們知道，連綿的天災人禍中
只有不停地繁殖生命
才能夠延續生命

*

吾皇出遊歐羅巴
應邀觀賞芭蕾舞劇《天鵝湖》
龍顏大悅
賞銀三千兩
返國後
仍念念不忘
遂傳旨太監
奔赴華夏各地
於窈窕三寸金蓮者中
甄選芭蕾舞娘
組建
皇家芭蕾舞團

this censure hasn't affected the Chinese breeding
if it weren't for revolutions, famines, wars,
plagues, popular movements, earthquakes,
floods, ligations, mine disasters,
the Chinese population
would be more than it is today

we know that the only way
to keep life going
through endless natural and man-made disasters
is to breed and breed

*

our emperor travelling in Europe
was invited to watch the ballet Swan Lake
his majesty was delighted
he awarded them three thousand catties of silver
back in his country
he couldn't forget about it
so he ordered eunuchs
to go all over China
to choose the ballet dancers
from pretty girls
with three-inch lotus feet
and so was formed
the royal ballet ensemble

*

大海，藍色的老虎
肆意咆哮
他想衝出巨大的籠子
籠子，不因為巨大
而不是籠子

而在那個遙遠的城市
一個從沒見過大海的人
徹夜擰開水龍頭
想以此
接通與大海的聯繫

*

飛機突然像帕金森患者一樣顫抖
我聽到機長的聲音：
「飛機正穿越氣流，請繫好安全帶！」
氣流之下，遼闊的西伯利亞
各種政治犯的流放地
列寧和史達林曾在這裏流放
但他們沒有死在此地
他們得以把自己的身體帶到莫斯科
為的是騰出西伯利亞的冰雪
冷藏更多的屍體

*

the sea, a big blue tiger
roar recklessly
He wants to get out of his big cage
a cage is still a cage
even if it's big

in a city far away
a man who has never seen sea
leaves the tap on
thinking that this
can connect him with the sea

*

the plane shook like someone
with Parkinson's disease
I heard the pilot:
"the plane is now passing through turbulence
please fasten your seat belts."
under the air vast Siberia
a place for every type of political exile
Lenin and Stalin were sent there once
but they didn't die there
they had to bring their bodies back to Moscow
so as to save the ice in Siberia
in order to freeze more corpses

*

里斯本，一個雨後的黃昏
在星星公園
在濕漉漉的花瓣間
他和一個叫久香的姑娘
不期而遇

她來自日本
她那櫻花一樣的微笑
讓他耳邊的盧溝橋槍聲
突然變得遙遠

*

養鳥的老人用一塊黑色的布
圍住鳥籠子
然後晃來晃去

他說，這是在模仿天空
在顛簸的黑暗中
鳥兒可以飛翔

*

Lisbon, an after-rain evening
in Jardim da Estrela
in the wet petals
he and a girl called Yuka Ezure
met

she was from Japan
her sakura smile
had that gunshot on the Marco Polo Bridge
resound so much further

*

the old man with the birds
used a black cloth
to cover the bird cage
and he rocked it

he said, this is like being in the sky
in the jerking darkness
the bird can fly

*

蘋果太甜
懷裏就會生出蟲子

如果讓愛情完整
就必須憂傷

電話線上的雨滴
變成了一千里的眼淚

三百畝的玫瑰
已經改種罌粟

*

麻雀需要天空
但不會翱翔雲天
牠們從屋簷跳到地上
一邊小心地覓食
一邊躲避着行人和車輛
灰頭土臉的牠們，常常
混同於塵土

牠們是離人類最近的鳥類
但只有天空和大地
可以養活牠們

*

an apple too sweet
would grow worms inside

sadness is necessary
to make love complete

raindrops on phone wires
became tears of a thousand miles

those acres of roses
are opium now

*

sparrows need the sky
but they don't soar
they jump from the roofs to the street
nimble for food
they hide from people and cars
their grey feathers
confused with dust

they're the birds closest to humans
but there's only the sky and earth
to raise them

籠子可以養活許多動物、鳥類，甚至人
但很難養活一只麻雀

*

翡冷翠的清晨
我坐在三樓的餐廳吃早餐
目光越過眼前的麵包和黃油
停留在窗前的繡球花上
再往前，看見對面的陽臺上
有一對年老的夫婦

晨光照在他們被時間蹂躪的臉上
遲緩的手
在風中抖開床單
抖開他們在上面種滿的鮮花

cages can provide for animals, birds, even humans
it's difficult to feed the sparrows

*

early morning in Florence
I had breakfast on the third floor of a restaurant
eyes skipped the bread and butter on the table
paused on the hydrangea by the window
then further
I saw on the opposite balcony
an old couple

morning shone on their time-trampled faces
their slow hands
shook the sheet in the wind
shook open the flowers they grew

*

其實，他根本沒病
他健康得甚麼都沒忘記
比如，不知從哪裏
他找到一頂警察的大簷帽
戴在了頭上
就立即有了威武的感覺
平時佝僂的身軀也挺立起來

他來到大街上
死死盯着往來的人群
看誰敢輕舉妄動
他突然有了抓人的衝動

*

孟德斯鳩説：人在苦難中
才活得像個人

其實恰恰相反，不知有多少人
在苦難中活成了動物

也許，孟德斯鳩所理解的苦難
和我所理解的苦難
並不一樣

*

actually, he's not sick
he's so healthy that he hasn't forgotten a thing
for example, not knowing where
he found a police cap
he put it on
and at once feels the might
his hunched body
straightened

he comes to the street
glares at pedestrians
sees who would take wild steps
he suddenly has the impulse
to arrest somebody

*

Montesquieu said: humans can only
live like humans in distress

actually it's the opposite, many end up
living like animals in distress

perhaps, the way Montesquieu understands distress
is different from mine

*

眼淚的配方，需有一截流水
但悲傷，或者快樂
要溶解多少鹽
才能製造出合格的淚水

淚水，記住多少難忘的時刻
要積攢多少重量
才會奪眶而出
漫過身體，加深大海的藍

而你，曾把一截流水
裝進舊瓶子
當成新酒向我出售

*

整條河流
整個大地
都被放在了手中

他把大地和河流
糅合在一起
摔打，揉捏
最後，他選擇最貧瘠的部分
塑出觀世音的慈顏

*

the formula of tears needs one part flowing water
but how much salt
should sadness or happiness dissolve
to produce proper tears

how many unforgettable moments
should tears record
and how much tearwater should accumulate
to rush from the eyes
over the body to deepen the blue of the sea

you once put a part of flowing water
into an old bottle
and sold it to me as new wine

*

the whole river
the whole land
placed in hands

he stuck the land
and the river together
beat and rubbed
at last he chose the most barren part
to mold the kind face of Kwan-yin

*

見到皇帝
人人都跪了下來

我卻勇敢地站了起來
為了跑到別人的前面
跪下來

*

我的畫家朋友
從無政府主義者蒲魯東那裏歸來
在白色的畫布上畫上了一片白色
白色上的白色
一個沒有政府的地方
一個樹比樹還高的地方

一幅畫就像是一張反對票
但不會取消皇帝
不會取消共和黨，不會取消民主黨
嘈雜的電視機裏
法案已經被橡皮通過了

於是，我的畫家朋友
在白色上的白色之上
又抹上一層白色

*

seeing the emperor
everyone knelt

but I bravely stood up
to get in a better kneeling spot
in front of the others' knees

*

my painter friend
back from the anarchist Proudhon's
painted white on a piece of white cloth
the white on white
place with no governance
a place where the trees are taller than trees

a painting is like a no vote
but it won't cancel out the king
the Republican and the Democratic parties
in the noisy television
bills have already been
passed by the eraser

so my painter friend
on the white on the white
painted white

*

五十年不變，不可能
一張臉用了五十年
皮肉和表情皆已鬆弛
這讓我顯得和善

青春期的憤怒，已過了保鮮期
變成肝鬱氣滯
遵中醫囑，吞服龍膽瀉肝丸
緊攥的拳頭漸漸鬆開了
綻放成兩朵鮮花

望遠鏡拉近遠方，折斷了目光
群山撞向頭顱
疼痛大聲呼喊
天空，巨大的消音器
吸收了所有的聲音

*

not a change for fifty years, no way
a face used for fifty years
flesh and facial expressions go flabby
that makes me look kind

rage of puberty, which has passed its expiry date
turns into liver-qi stagnation
taking the Chinese medicine doctor's advice
I swallow the dragon tea pills
tight fists gradually loosen
burst into two blossoms

using the telescope to bring the distance closer
and snap the survey
mountains hit my head
pain cries loudly
the sky is a muffler
absorbing all kinds of sounds

(Translated by Hilda Tam and Kit Kelen)

1958年生於北京，現居澳門，任教於澳門大學葡文系。發表過大量詩歌、翻譯和隨筆作品。著有中文和葡文詩集《寫在風的翅膀上》、《一條地平線，兩種風景》、《黑夜與我一起躺下》、《遠方之歌》、《當魚閉上眼睛》，譯作有《葡萄牙現代詩選》、《澳門中葡詩歌選》、《安德拉德詩選》、《中國當代十詩人作品選》等十餘部。2004年獲得第十四屆「柔剛詩歌獎」。2006年獲葡萄牙總統頒授「聖地亞哥寶劍勳章」。2009 年曾舉辦名為「於斯」的裝置展覽。

Yao Feng was born in Beijing but now lives in Macau. He is Associate Professor at the University of Macau's Portuguese Department. Yao has published widely in terms of poems, translation and prose. His books of Chinese and Portuguese poems include *Writing on the Wings of the Wind, One Horizon – Two Views, A Noite Deita-se Comigo, Faraway Song and When the Fish Close Their Eyes*. His books of translation include *Selecta de Poetas Portugueses Contemporâneos, Anthologie of Eugénio de Andrade and Um Barco Remenda o Mar*, etc. Yao was the winner of the 14th Rougang Poetry Award in 2004. In 2006, he was awarded Ordem Militar de Santiago de Espada medal by the President of Portugal and in 2009 he held the installation exhibition 'Belonging'.

出版 Publisher
香港中文大學出版社 The Chinese University Press

封面及平面設計 Cover and Graphic Designer
朱德華 Almond Chu

製稿及分色 Art Work and Colour Separation
明星鐳射分色有限公司 Star Laser Graphic Co. Ltd.

印刷 Printer
宏亞印務有限公司 Asia One Printing Ltd.

出版日期 Date of Publication
二零一一年十月 October 2011

國際書號 ISBN
978-962-996-529-7

香港國際詩歌之夜2011主辦單位
International Poetry Nights in Hong Kong 2011 Organizers

香港中文大學東亞研究中心
Centre for East Asian Studies, The Chinese University of Hong Kong

香港城市大學人文社會科學院
College of Liberal Arts and Social Sciences, City University of Hong Kong

香港科技大學人文社會科學學院
School of Humanities and Social Science,
The Hong Kong University of Science and Technology

香港國際詩歌之夜2011協辦單位
International Poetry Nights in Hong Kong 2011 Co-organizer
木刻文化出版有限公司 MUKE Publishing Limited